Ukulele for Seniors

www.melbay.com/21671BCDEB

by Joe Carr

Audio track listing

1. Tuning Notes
2. First Warm-Up
3. C Chord
4. C Chord Strum
5. *Brother John*
6. F Chord
7. *Row, Row, Row Your Boat*
8. Exercise
9. *Rock-a-My Soul*
10. C7 Chord
11. C7 Chord Exercise
12. *He's Got the Whole World in His Hands*
13. *Down in the Valley*
14. Rhythm Sheets
15. Rhythm Sheets 2
16. *Marianne*
17. *Will the Circle Be Unbroken?*
18. G Chord
19. G Exercise
20. Am Chord
21. Am Progression
22. Chord Progression

23. *This Little Light of Mine*
24. Amazing Grace
25. Two New Chords
26. Exercise
27. *This Train*
28. *Molly Malone*
29. Up Strum
30. Strum Pattern in 4/4
31. Exercise
32. *Oh Sinner Man*
33. Exercise
34. *Roll in my Sweet Baby's Arms*
35. Strum 3 Exercise
36. *When the Saints Go Marching In*
37. Up Strum Pattern
38. *Midnight Special*
39. 3/4 Strum Pattern
40. *Amazing Grace*
41. 3/4 Strum Pattern 2
42. *Silent Night*
43. New Chords
44. *Take Me Out to the Ballgame*

Contents adapted from Mel Bay's *Guitar for Seniors* by Mike Christiansen.
Special thanks to Gerald Jones for his playing on the accompanying audio.

Contents

Introduction

Congratulations on choosing the ukulele to play music! The ukulele or "uke" as it is commonly known, is an excellent choice for hands that are not as strong or as flexible as they may once have been. The fact that there are only four nylon strings to play makes the uke easier and faster to learn than its larger cousin - the guitar. We can start having fun making music right away!

This is a beginning ukulele method. The contents of this book present the fundamentals of playing ukulele in a sequence making the material logical and easy to learn. The primary differences between this method and others is that this book is written for seniors wanting to learn to play the ukulele. While many would say that getting on in years is only a state of mind, the fact is that some of the body parts (including the eyes) don't function quite the same as they did in younger years. With this in mind, the font has purposely been enlarged. Care has been taken to select repertoire familiar and appealing to a more mature audience and attention has been given to the pacing of the material.

Beginning senior students are to be complemented for studying the ukulele at this time in their life. It says a great deal about the person who is constantly exploring and learning. It is never too late to learn something new. In fact, the experience of years make seniors some of the best students.

-Joe Carr

Types of Ukuleles

The most common type ukulele is called the soprano ukulele. It is the smallest instrument in the uke family. The tenor uke and the concert uke are larger than the soprano but they are still tuned the same and use the same chords. The baritone uke is much larger and uses guitar tuning and chords. The chord shapes in this book will work for the baritone uke, but the letter names of the strings and chords are different.

Tuning

There are several methods that can be used to tune the ukulele. "My Dog Has Fleas" is a simple four note song used to help tune a ukulele when there is no other convenient note source available. To use this method, tune the fourth string to a note that matches the "My" note in your head making sure the string is neither too tight or too loose. Then tune the other strings carefully. Care must be taken in this method not to overstretch and break the strings. Beginners should use one of the methods below.

One of the easiest and most accurate tunimg methods is to use an electronic tuner. Electric tuners can be purchased at any music dealership and are safe and easy to use. Some have built-in microphones and some attach to the instrument (not permanently.) Those that attach to the instrument are useful because they leave your hands free, and the tuner will not pick up a lot of sounds other than your ukulele. The ukulele can also be tuned to a piano. The chart below shows the strings on the ukulele and the corresponding pitches to which they would be tuned on the piano.

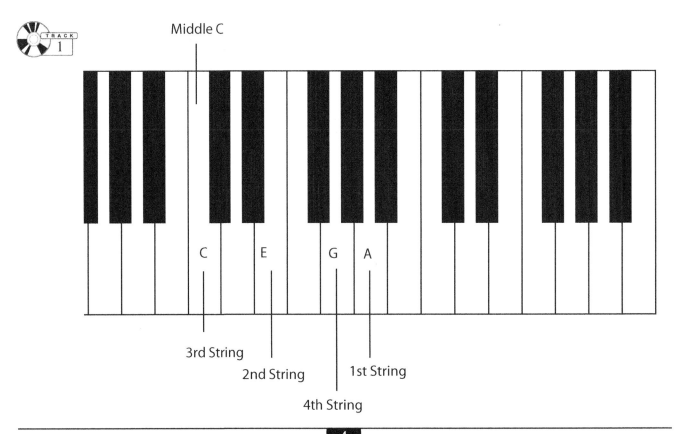

One of the simplest and most effective ways to tune a ukulele is to tune it to itself. If you have a piano or pitch pipe, tune the first string to the A above middle C. Then put a finger in the **fifth fret** on the **second string** and pick the second and first strings together; they should sound the same. If they do not, adjust the string which has a finger on it until the two strings match in pitch.

When the second string is in tune, place a finger in the **fourth fret** on the **third string**. Pick the third and the second string together. If they do not sound the same, adjust the third string which is the string with the finger on it. When these two strings sound the same, match the fourth string to the first by placing a finger in the **second fret** on the **fourth string** and match it to the first string open.

After all of this is done, strum several chords and see if the chords sound in tune. If they don't sound quite right, repeat the process and if it still does not help, something may be wrong with the instrument itself. The frets may be misplaced or the bridge of the ukulele may need some adjusting. If so, take the instrument to a qualified repairperson or to an instructor (a guitar instructor will do) and let him adjust the instrument.

You may also tune each string on the ukulele to pitches on the piano. If this method is used, tune the first string open (without any fingers on the string) to A above middle C on the piano. The second string is tuned to E above middle C. The third string is tuned to middle C. The fourth string is tuned to G above middle C. Strum each string from the fourth through the first to hear the familiar *My Dog Has Fleas* melody.

The ukulele may also be tuned to a tuning fork. A tuning fork may be purchased that sounds an A note. Tap the tuning fork and touch it to the bridge of the ukulele. The sound which resonates will be the pitch you match to the first string. Then proceed as you did in the self tuning paragraph above.

First Warm Up

To become familiar with the feel of the ukulele and to develop coordination, play the following warm-up exercise.

Step 1 - Begin by playing the first string open. Open means no left-hand fingers are pushing on the string.

Step 2 - Next, play the first string, first fret. The left-hand first finger should be pushing on the string.

Step 3 - Next play the first string, second fret. The second finger should be used to push on the second fret.

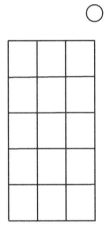

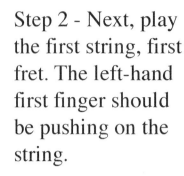

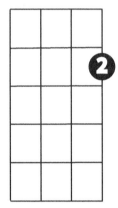

Step 4 - Next, play the first string, third fret, using the second finger.

Step 5 - Next, play the first string, fourth fret using the third finger.

Step 6 - Finally, play the first string, fifth fret, using the left-hand fourth finger.

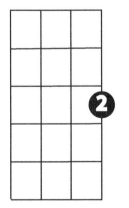

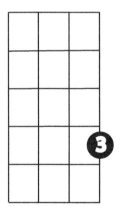

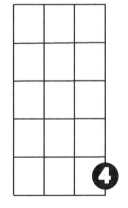

Now play these same notes in reverse order (5-4-3-2-1), still on the first string. Repeat this exercise several times up and down the fingerboard. After doing the exercise several times on the first string, repeat the same sequence on each string.

Chord Diagrams

Drawn below is a diagram of the ukulele neck. These diagrams are commonly used to illustrate the fingers for chords. A chord is produced when three or more strings are played together. The verticle lines represent the strings with the first string to the far right. The horizontal lines represent the frets. The top fret line is the nut. The dots represent where to place the left-hand fingers. The numbers on the dots indicate which left-hand finger to use. The circles above the diagram indicate open strings to be played. Open strings are those that do not have left-hand fingers pressing on them. An "X" above a string on the diagram indicates that the string is not to be played. Diamond shaped dots indicate root notes - a C note in the case of the C chord below.

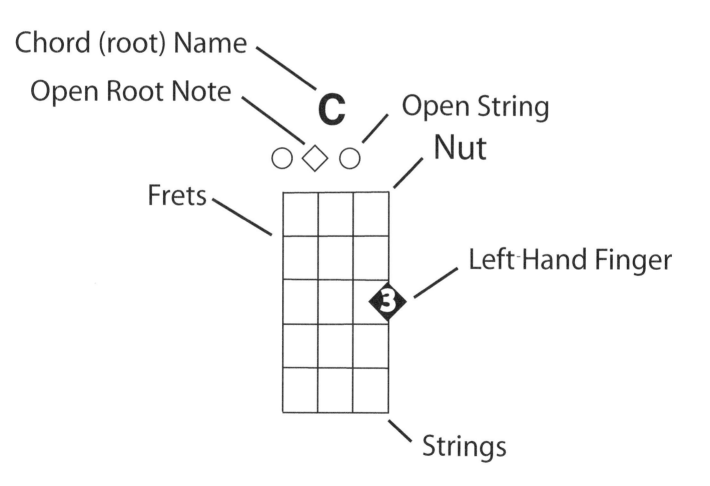

First Chords

The first chord to be presented is the C chord. As shown on the diagram below, this chord is played by placing the left-hand third finger on the first string in the third fret. All four strings are strummed. As you can see, strings two, three and four are played open along with the fretted first string. Strum this chord down several times.

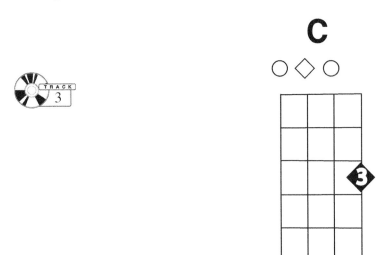

These slash marks (/) are called strum bars. They indicate to strum a chord down one time. Each strum bar gets one beat. Be sure to use a straight downward motion using the right-hand thumb.

Practice the following exercise strumming the C chord the number of times indicated by the strum bars. After strumming the C chord four times, play four strings open.

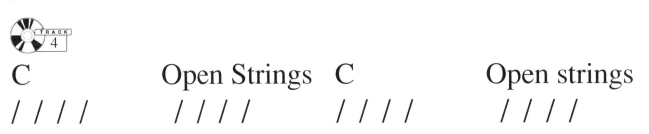

C	Open Strings	C	Open strings
/ / / /	/ / / /	/ / / /	/ / / /

The following song can be accompanied by strumming only one chord; C. Play the C chord one time for each bar strum and sing the melody. Some strums do not have a word underneath and sometimes there are two syllables to a strum bar.

Brother John

C

/ / / / / / / / / / / / / /

Are you sleep-ing? Are you sleep-ing? Bro-ther John,   Bro-ther John

/ / / / / / / / / / / /

Morn-ing bells are ring-ing! Morn-ing bells are ring-ing! Ding-Ding Dong

/ / / /

Ding-Ding Dong

The next chord to be learned is the F chord. Practice playing the F chord several times.

F

   The next song uses only the F chord. Strum the F chord one time for every strum bar. Keep the strums even. Be sure to strum the chord when the word under the strum bar is sung.

Row, Row, Row Your Boat

F

/ / / / / / / /

Row, row. row your boat gent-ly down the stream

/ / / / / / / /

Mer-ri-ly, mer-ri-ly, mer-ri-ly, mer-ri-ly life is but a dream.

The next exercise and song use the C and F chords. Practice changing the chords quickly and smoothly. To reach the point where the chords can be changed quickly, change from one chord to the next and keep the right-hand strumming. Eventually, the right hand will force the left-hand to change quickly.

TRACK 8

C   **F**   **C**
/ / / / / / / /   / / / / / / / /   / / / / / / / /

F   **C**   **F**
/ / / / / / / /   / / / /   / / / /

C   **F**   **C**
/ / / /   / / / /   / / / /

TRACK 9

Rock - A - My Soul

F
/   /   /   /   /   / /   /
Rock-a-my soul in the bosom of A-bra-ham.

C
/   /   /   /   /   / /   /
Rock-a-my soul in the bosom of A-bra-ham.

F
/   /   /   /   /   / /   /
Rock-a-my soul in the bosom of A-bra-ham.

C   **F**
/   /   /   /   /   /   /   /
Oh. _____ Rock-a-my soul_____

The next chord to learn is the C7 shown below. Practice the song after the exercise. The song contains the F and C7 chords. Strum each chord one time for each strum bar.

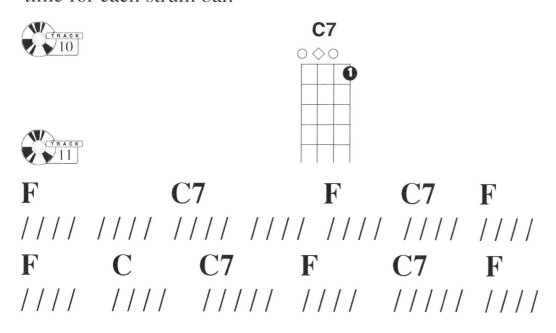

C7

F   **C7**   **F**   **C7**   **F**

/ / / /   / / / /   / / / /   / / / /   / / / /   / / / /   / / / /

F   **C**   **C7**   **F**   **C7**   **F**

/ / / /   / / / /   / / / / /   / / / /   / / / / /   / / / /

He's Got the Whole World in His Hands

F

/ / /   /   /   /   /   /   /   /

He's got the whole world in His hands, He's got the
He's got the little bitty baby, etc.
He's got you and me brother, etc.

C7   **F**

/   / / /   / /   /   /   / / / /

whole world in His hands, He's got the whole world

                        C7   **F**

/   /   /   /   /   /   / /   / / / /

in His hands. He's got the whole world in His hands,

Rhythm Sheets

A rhythm sheet is a type of written music that shows the lyrics to a song, the chords above the lyrics and a fraction at the beginning of the song (i.e. 4/4 or 3/4) called the time signature. Only be concerned with the top number in the time signature. The top number indicated how many times to strum each chord name. For example, in *Down in the Valley*, because the top number in the time signature is three, strum each chord name three times. Use only down strums.

Down in the Valley

3/4

F	F	F	F	C7	C7
/	/	/			

1. Down in the val-ley   valley so low   Hang your head
2. Build me a cas-tle   fourty feet high   So I can
3. Write me a let-ter   send it by mail   Send it in

C7 C7	C7	F	F

o-ver.   Hear the wind   blow.
see him   as he rides   by.
care of   Birming-ham   jail.

Measured Music

The five lines and four spaces in standard notation music is callled a staff. Ukulele music is generally written in music with a treble clef sign (see below in first staff) at the beginning of the music. The staff is divided into sections with bar lines. The sections between the bar lines are called measures. Inside of each measure, there are a specific number of beats. A beat is the pulse of the music or a measurement of time. Next to the treble clef sign is a fraction called a time signature. The top number of the time signature indicates how many beats are in each measure.

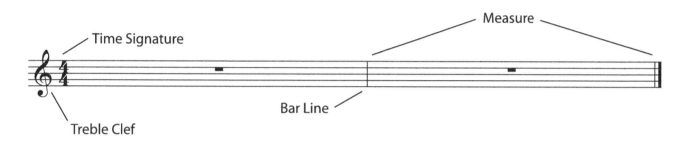

When playing rhythm for accompaniment, strum the chord written above the measure once for each beat in the measure. Strum down with the right-hand thumb. In 4/4 time, strum down four times for each measure. In 3/4 time, strum down three times in each measure. If a C is written where the time signature would appear, this stands for 4/4 or common time. If a C with a line through it is written, this is cut time (2/2) and the chords should be strummed two times in each measure.

Practice the following exercises and songs strumming down in the measures.

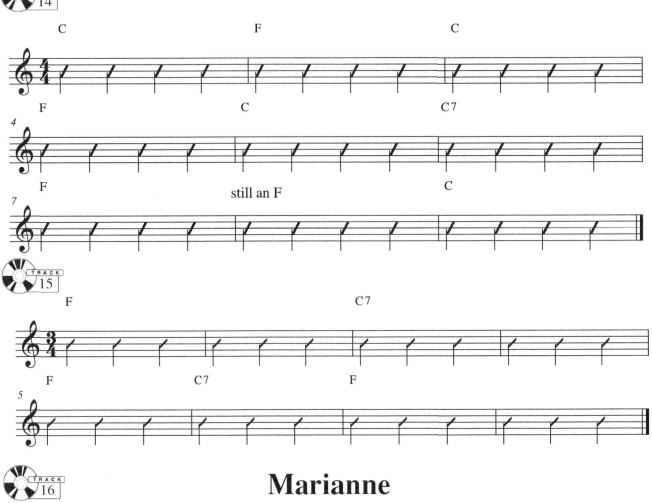

Marianne

Remember to strum four times in a measure.

Practice the following songs using down strums.

Will the Circle be Unbroken?

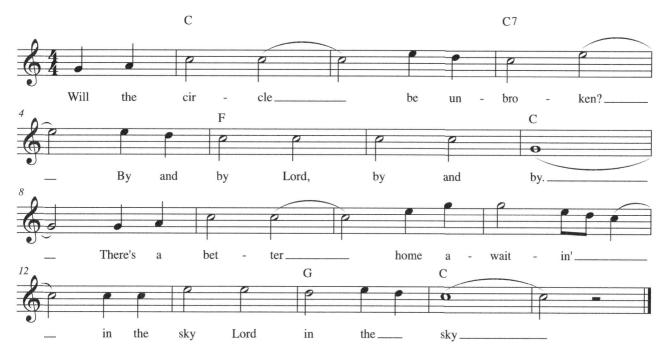

Will the cir - cle ____ be un - bro - ken? ____

__ By and by Lord, by and by. ____

__ There's a bet - ter ____ home a - wait - in' ____

__ in the sky Lord in the ____ sky ____

The G Chord

The chord drawn below is a G chord. The first three fingers of the left-hand are used and all four strings are strummed.

TRACK 18

TRACK 19

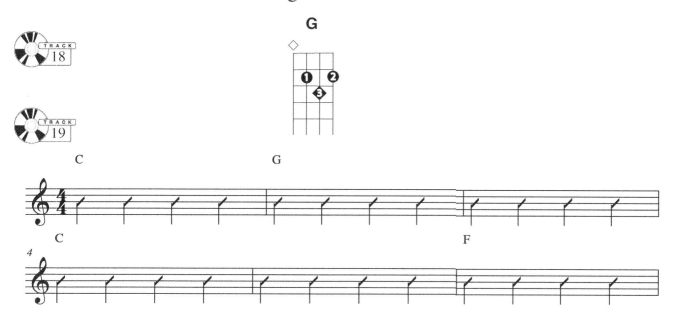

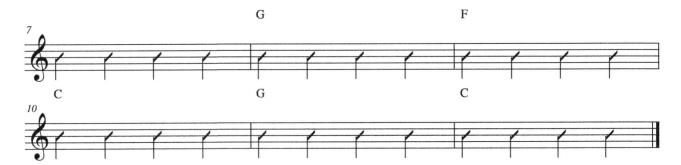

The A Minor (Am) Chord

The chord drawn below in an A minor chord. Minor chords are written with an "m" or a "-" (minus) sign next to the chord letter name. The A minor chord uses the left-hand second finger.

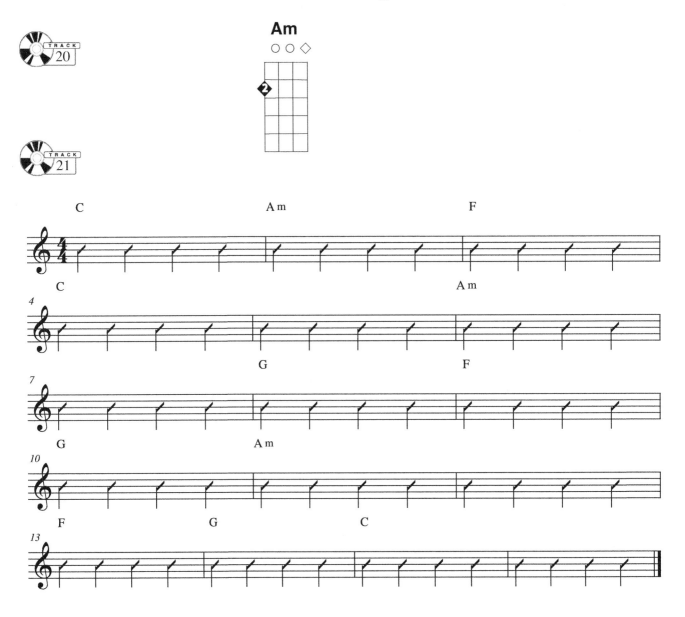

A *chord progression* is a series of chords. The following chord progression contains an A minor chord and is commonly found in Spanish music.

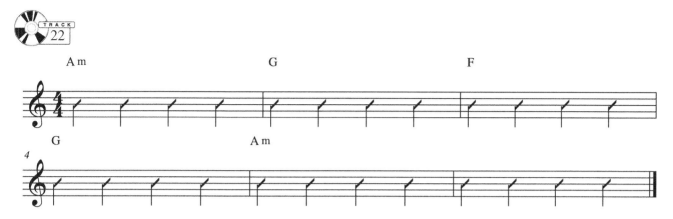

Practice the following songs that contain the chords presented so far. If the song is in 4/4. strum down four times a measure. If the song is in 3/4 strum down three times in each measure.

This Little Light of Mine

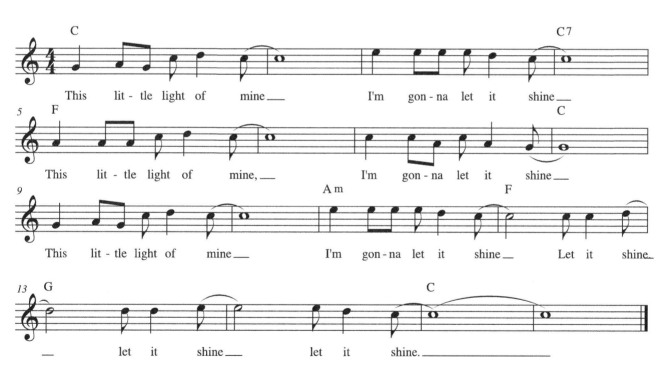

Amazing Grace

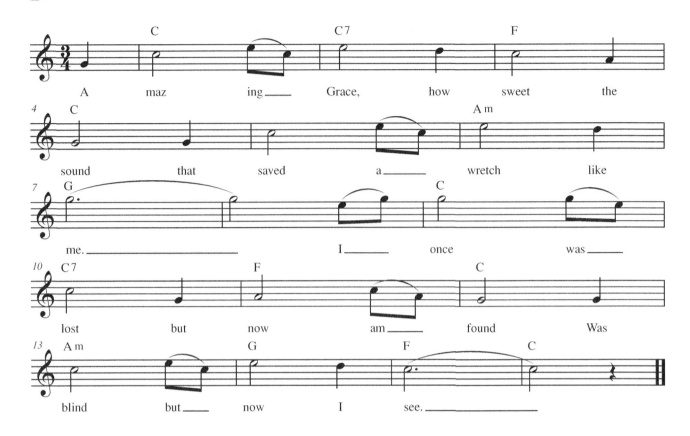

Two New Chords

Drawn below are the Dm and G7 chords. Practice them individually and then play the exercise and songs containing these new chords. Notice when changing from the an F to a Dm chord, the left-hand first and second fingers remain in the same position. Also when changing Dm or F to the G7 chord, the left-hand first finger remains in the same position. Fingers that remain in the same place when chords change are called *pivot fingers*.

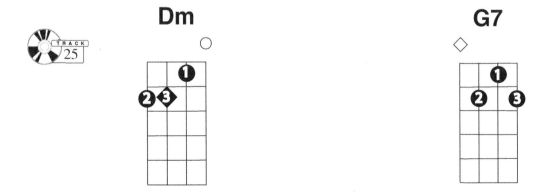

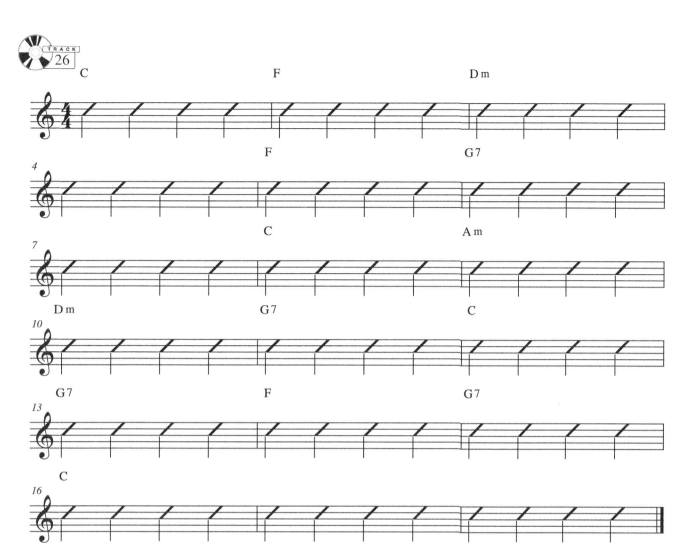

This Train

This train is bound for glo-ry, this train _____

This train is bound for glo-ry, this train! _____

This train is bound for glo-ry, don't take none but the good and Ho - ly.

This train is bound for glo-ry, this train! _____

Molly Malone

In Dub - lin's fair cit - y where girls are so pret - ty, oh

there's where I met my sweet Mol - ly Ma - lone. And she

wheeled her wheel - bar - row through the streets broad and nar - row, cry - ing

"Cock - les and mus - sels, a - live, a - live - o." "A -

live, a - live o. _____ a - live a - live o." _____ cry - ing

"Cock - les and mus - sels a - live a - live - o."

Up Strum

When strumming a chord with an up stroke, regardless of the chord being played, strum only two or three strings with the up stroke. The up strum is executed with an up and slightly outward motion. The bracket shown over the first note in the example below is used to indicate a down stroke. The "v" sign is used to indicate an up stroke. Generally, when two strum bars are connected with a beam, there are two strums on one beat. The first comes on the first half of the beat and is played with a down stroke. The second is played on the second half of the beat and is played using an up stroke. The down stroke is counted as the beat on which it occurs, and the up stroke is counted as "and." Practice the following exercise strumming each chord as indicated.

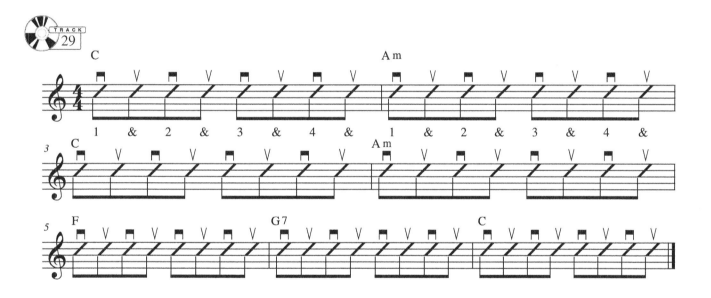

Strum Patterns for 4/4

The simplest strum pattern for 4/4 (strumming down four times in each measure) was presented earlier. The simplest pattern for 3/4 is to strum down three times in each measure. Although these patterns are easy to execute, when used in the right song, they can be effective. This section of the book will present several strum patterns that use combinations of down and up strums. By combining down and up strums, interesting accompaniment patterns can be created. An exercise and a song will be given to apply each strum pattern. Each pattern can be used to play any song in 4/4. The strums patterns presented here can be applied to sheet music and songbooks as well as the songs in this book. Generally, once a pattern has been selected, the same pattern is used in each measure throughout the song. The strum pattern written below take one measure in 4/4 to complete. Reminders of the strum direction are written above the strum bars, and the rhythm is written below. Hold any chord and practice this strum pattern.

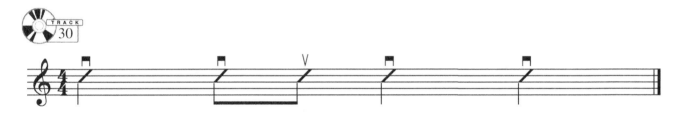

Practice the following exercises and song using the strum pattern written above or in the first measure. Use the same strum pattern to play in every measure.

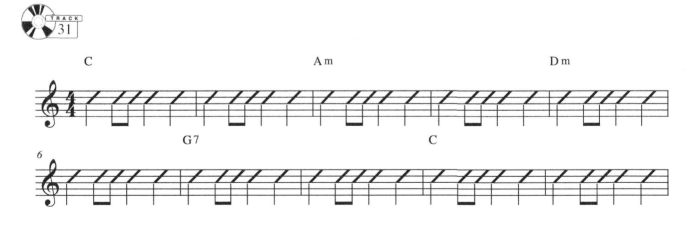

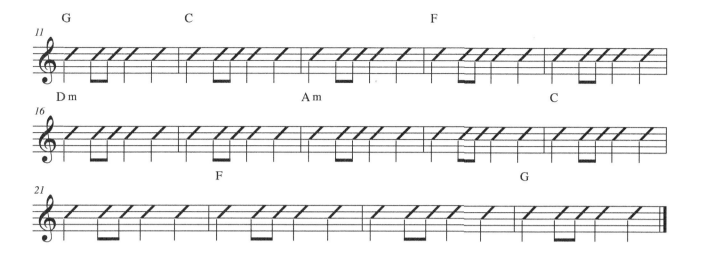

When playing the chords, do not be concerned with the notes, but rather the chords, how many beats are in each measure, and how many measures the chord gets. Use the same strum pattern in each measure.

Oh, Sinner Man

Written below is another strum that works to play songs in 4/4. After practicing the strum pattern holding any chord, apply the strum pattern to the exercise and song that follows.

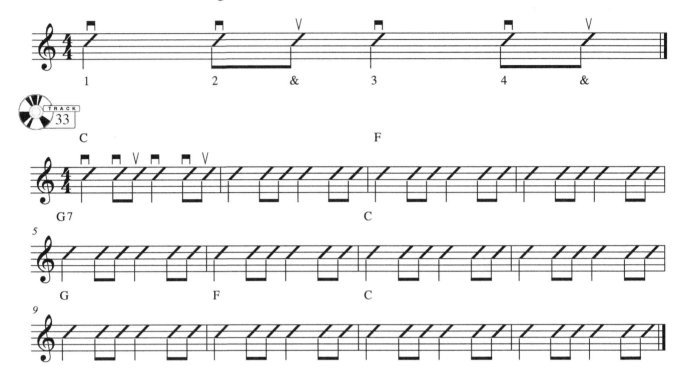

Roll in my Sweet Baby's Arms

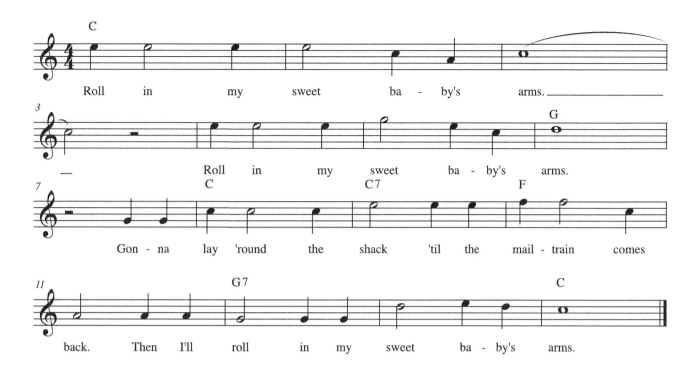

Roll   in   my   sweet   ba - by's   arms.

— Roll   in   my   sweet   ba - by's   arms.

Gon - na   lay   'round   the   shack   'til   the   mail - train   comes

back.   Then   I'll   roll   in   my   sweet   ba - by's   arms.

Here is another strum that works well for 4/4. Practice this strum pattern and the exercise and song.

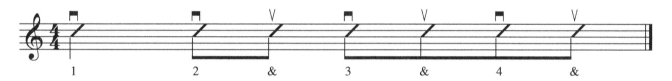

1   2   &   3   &   4   &

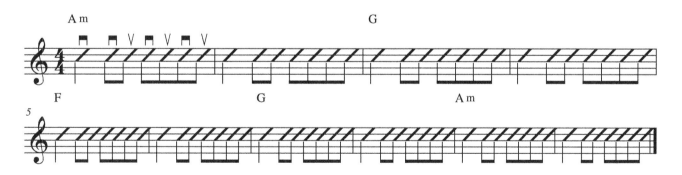

When the Saints Go Marching In

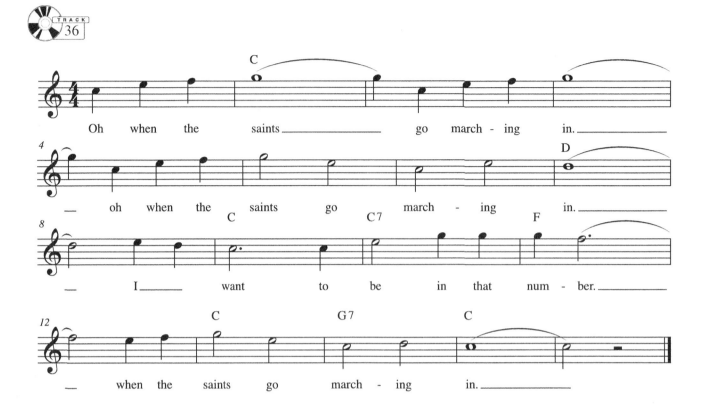

A loop that connects two strum bars is called a *tie*. When the tie is written, play the strum bar at the left of the tie. but do not play the strum bar connected on the right side of the tie. Instead, allow the strum at the first of the tie to ring through the strum bar connected with the tie.

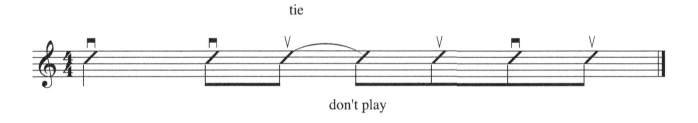

This strum pattern can be used to play songs in 4/4. It is a bit tricky because of the tie. There are two up strums together in the middle of the pattern with a pause between them (where the other down strum would have been.) Remember, when strumming up, play only two or three strings.

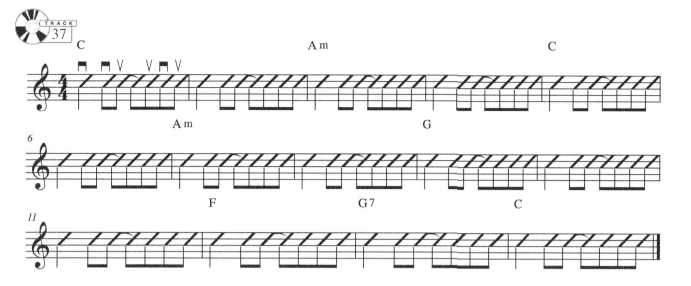

Repeat Sign

The song *Midnight Special* contains a repeat sign. When a repeat sign. :‖ , is written, go from that spot in the music to where the repeat sign with the dots on the right, ‖: is written in the music and play that portion again. The song may be repeated once or as many times as it takes to sing all the verses. Practice strumming the following song.

Midnight Special Blues

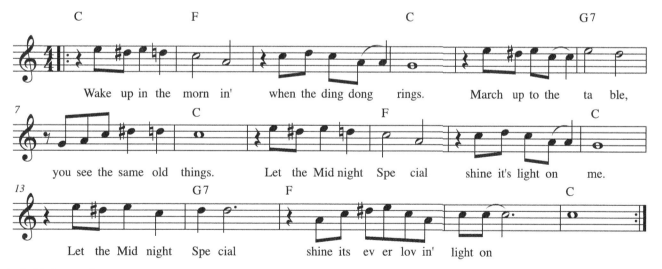

Additional verse:

2. There upon the table
Knife and fork and pan,
Say a word about it
There's trouble with the man.

Strum Patterns for 3/4

The strum patterns in this section of the book can be used to play songs in 3/4 or waltz time. Each pattern is presented with an exercise and a song. Each pattern takes one measure to complete. Like the patterns in 4/4, once a pattern has been selected, use the same pattern in each measure. Also, like the 4/4 patterns, the 3/4 patterns are listed in order of difficulty. Hold any chord at first while learning each pattern.

The following pattern contains one up strum. First, play the pattern holding any chord. Then, play the exercise and song.

Amazing Grace

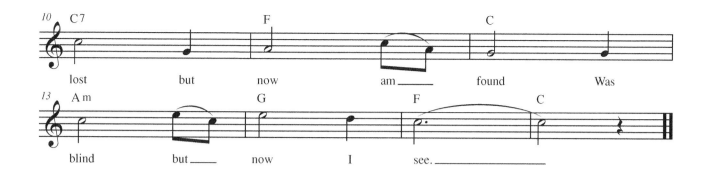

lost   but   now   am____   found   Was

blind   but____   now   I   see.____

Here is another strum pattern for 3/4.

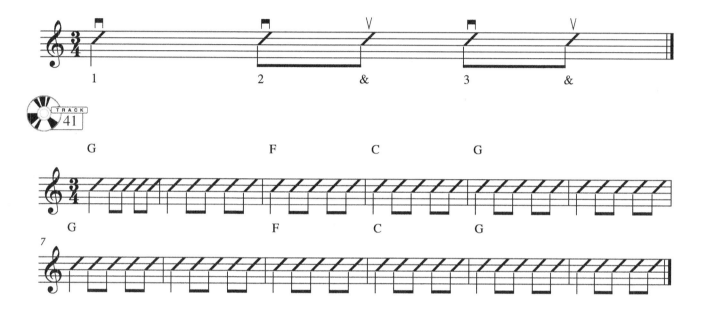

After practicing this new strum pattern for 3/4 and the followng exercise, return to the songs presented earlier in this section of the book that used strum patterns for 3/4 and apply this new pattern to each measure.

Remember, the strum patterns for 4/4 and 3/4 can be applied to songs written in sheet music or songbooks.

Silent Night

Si lent night, ho ly night,

All is calm, all is bright.

Round yon vir gin moth er and child.

Ho ly in fant so ten der and mild.

Sleep in heav en ly peace

Sleep in heav en ly peace.

Additional Verse:

2. Silent night, holy night,
   Shepherds quake at the sight.
   Glories stream from heaven afar,
   Heavenly hosts sing Alleluia,
   Christ the Savior in born!
   Christ the Savior in born!

New Chords D7 and A7 and F# Dim

Practice the D7, A7 and F# diminished chords drawn on the diagrams below. Notice there are two fingerings given for the D7 and A7. The fingering on the left is easier, but practice both. In the diagram of the D7 on the right, the three number ones indicate that the first finger lays across (or barres) strings two, three and four. Any of the strum patterns for 3/4 may be used.

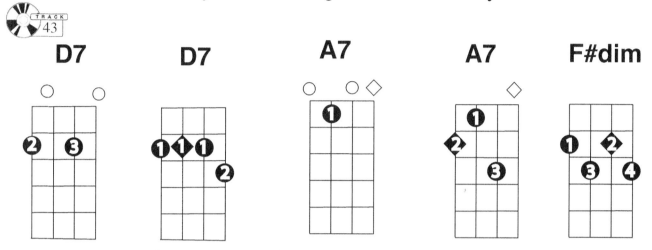

Take Me Out to the Ballgame

Words by Jack Norworth, Music by Albert Von Tilzer

About the Author

Photo by Gerald Jones.

Since 1985, Joe Carr has been a music instructor specializing in Bluegrass, Western Swing and Irish music in the Commercial Music program at South Plains College in Levelland, Texas. He is a director for Camp Bluegrass, a summer residential Music camp in its 24th year (2010).

In 1977, Joe joined the internationally known *Country Gazette* bluegrass band with banjo player Alan Munde and bluegrass legend Roland White. Joe appeared on three group albums, a solo album and numerous other recorded projects during his seven-year tenure with the band. In the 1990s, Carr and Munde formed a duo that toured extensively throughout the U.S., Canada and England and recorded two albums for Flying Fish/Rounder Records.

Joe has developed and appeared in instructional music videos for Mel Bay Publications. He has written many instructional book/audio combinations for Mel Bay and has a growing number of videos available.

Joe is a regular columnist for *Flatpicking Guitar Magazine* and *Mandolin Magazine* and is a periodic contributor to *Fiddler Magazine*. He is the editor for Mel Bay's webzine Mandolin Sessions: www.mandolinsessions.com

Printed in Great Britain
by Amazon

24060316R00020